Prediction Stories

Revised Edition

Jacquelyn Hester Colleton-Akins

ISBN: Softcover   978-1-7960-4067-8
         EBook   978-1-7960-4066-1

Print information available on the last page

Rev. date: 06/14/2019

To order additional copies of this book, contact:
Xlibris
1-888-795-4274
www.Xlibris.com
Orders@Xlibris.com

To my parents, Peter and Ruby Hester. I love you.

In the year 1955, I lived in Jacksonville, Florida, on the west side in a section called Mixson Town on McCoy Boulevard. Our house centered in front of McCoy Creek. The house we lived in was white and green with a big front porch with a swing, and a big back porch. Mother built a barbeque grill in the center of the porch. I would say my home was an ideal place to grow up in with my uncle and sister. My uncle, Henry; my sister, Sue Ann; and I shared the same bedroom. My bed was right beside a window big enough for me to climb into and sit and gaze out. I just loved looking out the window at the rain in the daylight and nighttime; it made me feel so good inside. On a hot Thursday day, my uncle, sister, and I would always ask each other what kind of story Daddy would tell us on Friday.

Henry said, "I hope he would tell us a scary, scary, story."

Sue Ann said, "I hope Daddy tells us about when he was a little boy or about when he was a singer."

I said, "Let it be funny and not scary."

My uncle replied, "I hope it be scary so Jacquelyn will be afraid to go to the bathroom and she will wet the bed again, Hahaha!"

I said, "I'm telling Momma that you are frightening me."

It was Friday. I jumped out of my bed and ran to my window to look out to see what the weather would be like. "Oh my, today will be a beautiful day."

Then Momma called, "Jacquelyn, Sue Ann, and Henry, time for breakfast!"

Sue Ann said, "Today is Friday. We get pancakes."

Momma said, "Yes, today is pancake day. Children, today is Friday. I will be turning the television off at two p.m."

Henry said, "Ruby, it's summertime. Can we keep the television on?"

My mother replied, "No, you may not. Now go outside and play while I prepare lunch and dinner."

The family looked forward to being entertained with a good story from Daddy.

It was now 7:00 p.m., time for Daddy to come home from work; it was time to eat dinner.

Henry said, "Ruby always cooked a good dinner on Friday night."

Sue Ann stated, "It's only fish and potato salad."

Then I stated, "And blueberry cobbler and strawberry ice cream. Yummy!"

During this time, I was only five years old; I was reading big books and writing stories.

After we completed our dinner, Mother said, "Let's move into the den."

Then Daddy yelled out, "Ruby! Prepare the lemonade and some buttery popcorn." During this time relaxing in the den, my daddy stated, "Bring a pen, a pencil, and a piece of paper with you."

My uncle Henry yelled out, "Jacquelyn, don't forget your fat pencil and cornbread paper!"

At the stroke of nine o'clock, my daddy began telling us to keep in mind all his stories were categorized: number 1, childhood stories; number 2, dead-peoples stories; number 3, family life stories; and number 4, prediction stories.

My daddy stated, "There will be prediction stories for each one of you." My daddy, Peter, began saying to Henry, "Right after you completed high school, you will go into a war called Vietnam War. This war will take you on a journey in a far country. Henry, you will have good success being in the army. You will serve many years and come out of the war in good standard." My daddy kept telling Henry, "Jesus will be with you all the way." My daddy stated to my uncle, "You will be a journalist working with newspapers. You will work as a janitor before you become a journalist."

My daddy stated to Sue Ann, "Your first love will cause you to be pregnant with a baby girl. You will get married to an older gentleman. From this older gentleman, you will conceive four babies. Later in the marriage, you will discover James is still married to his first wife. You will work at a hospital as an IV therapist, and from this job, you will work many years and retire from this job."

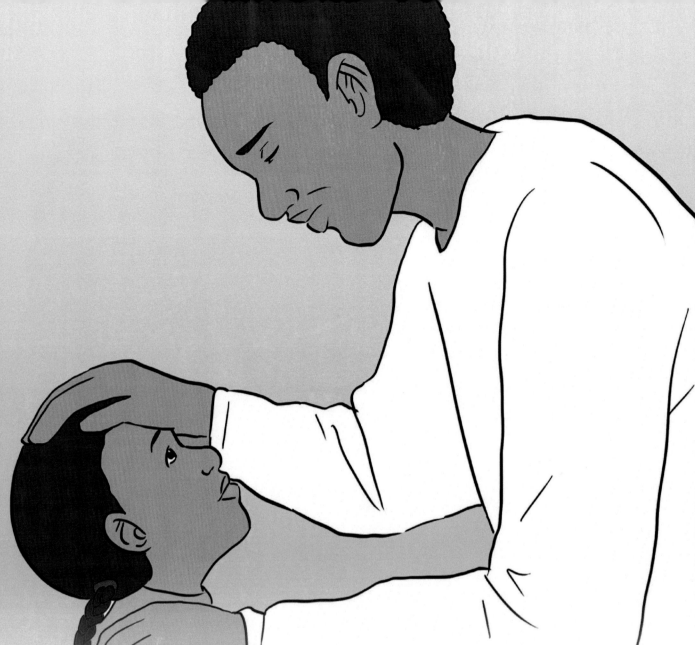

My daddy stated, "Jacquelyn, you will get married twice in life. You will be the first one to achieve a higher education before your siblings. You will receive many degrees and licenses. Your first teaching job will cost you lots of pain and suffering, because you will be opening doors for other blacks to work in the school system. Jacquelyn, you will also be a nurse working with all kinds of peoples." Then he said, "Jacquelyn, you have the gift to be a writer. Your writing skills will take you through all kinds of adventures. I have some more for you, Jacquelyn, concerning your writing. I see a skinny black man with initials BO. This man will be the first black president, a Democrat. He will be hated by some Republicans, refusing to pass different laws." Then suddenly, my daddy put his right hand on my head and said, "Here she comes, the one that will follow after the black man. This woman will be a white woman of God, a Democrat. She loves all races of people, and she will be a just person for all mankind. She will have difficulty running to be the president." My daddy yelled out, "Jacquelyn, I only see her initials, HC!"

Then my daddy collapsed on the floor, and then all of us picked him up and put him on the sofa. My mother put a cold compress on his forehead; he began to come to. It was after twelve o'clock, and my mother said it was time to go to bed.

My daddy said, "Don't go to bed, not yet. HC will get married to a man who will be the president of the United States. There will be a young lady who will try to bring HC's husband down. This young lady will almost get him impeached from his presidential job. HC's husband will be a man of God. He will have dignity, integrity, and honor. He will fall in love with HC at first sight. This man of God will never, never break his love for HC. HC will be running against a man from her past. She called him a friend/associate in the past. Later, this man will be her adversary. HC is called many names by this devil adversary. HC will be able to prevail throughout her walk to the White House as being the first female president."

We observed Daddy beginning to perspire all over and shaking, then he said, "I must rest."

Henry, Sue Ann, and I kissed our parents good night and went to our room. We slept in the same room, but we had different beds.

The three of us were very quiet, then my uncle said, "I wonder what kind of drink my brother had before he came home."

Sue Ann said, "You know Daddy like to drink gin sometimes."

With me being five years old, I was still looking at all this like a bedtime story. After, we settled down and went to sleep.

The next morning, I took out my journal and began writing down what my daddy prophesied.

Sue Ann, Henry, and I went through the whole week having mixed feelings about Friday night story time. My daddy came home on Friday at the same time, and he turned on the television and said, "Ruby, call me when dinner is ready."

During dinnertime, my daddy never said anything, and we were afraid to say anything to him about story time. After dinner, he went to the den, reclined in his favorite reclining chair, and went to sleep. Henry, Sue Ann, and I observed Daddy was not the same anymore. He began to consume gin, two pints a day. Five months had passed.

Henry, Sue Ann, and I moved on in life and grew up. In 1969, Mother and Daddy were living apart. Our family size grew. Georg Ann died from the yellow fever. We moved from out of our home and moved into the apartments on Jefferson Street. Mother began receiving welfare, only eighty dollars a month to live on. We moved around a lot. My brothers and sisters and I survived the difficulty in life, and we had to grow, develop, mature, and be spiritual in Jesus Christ in order to survive the ghetto.

Sue Ann, in the tenth grade, met her first love. She fell in love with this man. During this time, we were living on a street called Madison Street. Henry would always say to Sue Ann, "You getting fat, and you throwing up your food each time you eat. You need to tell Momma that you are sick."

Sue Ann would reply, "I'm not sick. Just leave me alone."

I observed Sue Ann was sleeping a lot, not going to school, and meaner than a junkyard dog. Meanwhile, time had passed. I observed Sue Ann getting sick and having pains in her abdomen. Momma rushed Sue Ann to Duval Medical Center Hospital that night. She gave birth to a baby girl; she named her Lisa. Lisa's daddy was named Fermon. He never took time to support or be a daddy to Lisa.

Henry shouted out when Sue Ann brought her baby home three days later, "My brother prediction came true!"

Sue Ann started crying. "I know, I know, I know." Sue Ann dropped out of school in the tenth grade. A close friend of Sue Ann from her school days fell in love with baby Lisa and wanted to be her father. At the age of five years old, Lisa was adopted by James. He became her father; he had been taking care of Lisa throughout her life until he passed away.

Sue Ann began working at a day care and a preschool as a teacher's aide. Then at night, she went back to school, completing high school.

Sue Ann met another older man named James Thompson. This man swept Sue Ann off her feet. She was so in love with this man she just believed everything he said to her, and then in about three months, she was pregnant again; they got married. We were very happy for her, and we liked James. He moved Sue Ann in his beautiful home. Everything was just going all right.

Sue Ann had three more babies from James. James was a good provider, and Sue Ann was so happy.

Seven years passed by, and life was still good to Sue Ann. In the month of June 1973, Sue Ann received a telephone call from a strange lady with a hoarse voice, stating, "Get out of my home. I will be coming home, and take all of your children with you."

When James came home from work that day, Sue Ann questioned James about this lady. Sue Ann asked James for his divorce papers from his wife; James was unable to provide the divorce papers. James began saying to Sue Ann, "My wife had a stroke, and she was put in a nursing home. I found out two days ago she had recovered. My wife will be discharged tomorrow. She wants to come live in her home."

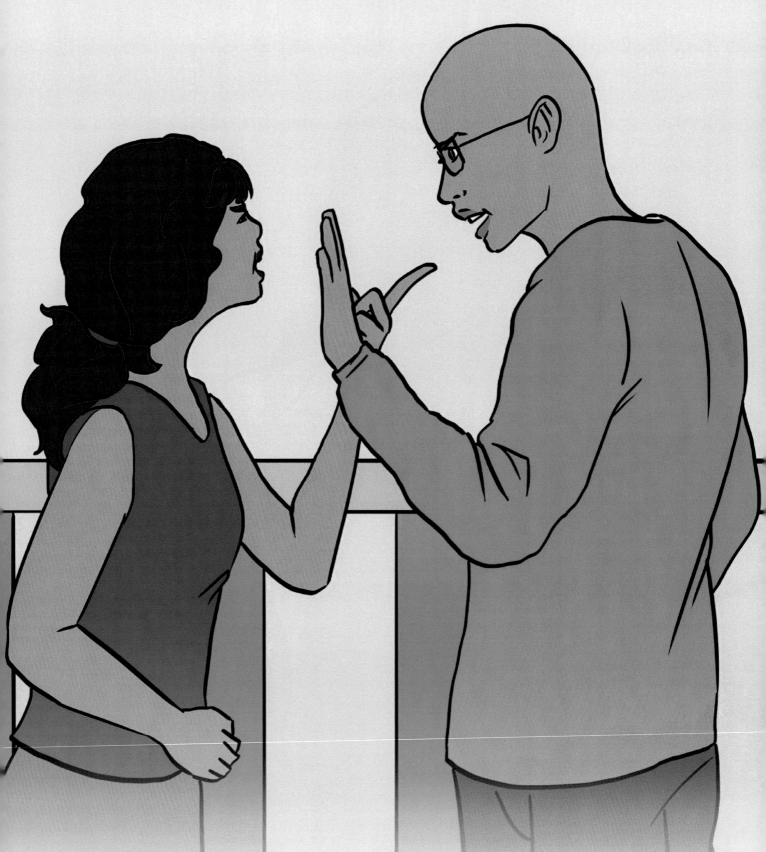

Sue Ann began arguing and crying, saying, "We are married, and we have three children together." Sue Ann stated, "We are not legally married, and your name is on each child's birth certificate."

Later that day, James got Sue Ann an apartment on Eighth and Davis Street. Our daddy's prediction came true again.

Sue Ann survived; she went on and became an IV therapist at Shands Hospital off Eighth Street. She worked there for many years with good success. She purchased a beautiful home and car, then later she retired after many years of service as an IV therapist. Daddy's prediction came true.

My uncle Henry served many years in the army. He retired highly decorated with medals. His brother's prediction came true. Henry kept moving up in life; he landed a position as a custodian and then moved into the newscast room, where he received training as a journalist. Uncle Henry Hester began working as a journalist. He was the first African American to obtain a journalism position at *St. Pittsburgh Times* newspaper in St. Pittsburgh, Florida.

I remember that night very clearly when I was five years old, after my daddy collapsed from giving us the shock of our lives. Over the years, I was unable to complete this story because I had to wait and see if it came to pass.

I did attend a junior college and later transferred to Florida Agricultural Mechanical University, and I majored in three different curriculums, and I was successful. I earned my BS degree in the year 1980. I was the first sibling to reach this goal. My daddy's predictions came true. I went on to other colleges, like Edward Waters College, and I specialized in special education in elementary through senior high school and completed it in 1999. My daddy's predictions came true.

My first teaching position was in Jacksonville, Florida, in the Duval County school board.

I was married to an older gentleman for fifteen years, and the marriage ended in a divorce. I got married a second time to a younger man for thirty years, and then the marriage ended in a divorce. My daddy's prediction came true.

I am at my computer, reading over this long life stories, telling myself I am waiting to see the outcome. I have been praying all my life. I will run on and see what the Lord has in store for me. My daddy predicted she will come with power and authority, with the initials HC. She is a Caucasian woman and will be the next president. I am waiting for my daddy's prediction to come true on this statement. Her husband did become the president of the United States. My daddy's prediction came true. A woman did try to bring HC's husband down or to be impeached. He was not impeached, and my daddy's prediction came true.

I left this part for the conclusion. The skinny black man will be educated, a man of God, with dignity and honor, a just man who loves all mankind and obeys the Ten Commandments in the Holy Bible, a man that loves his family. This man served two terms as our president, and he showed the world the most powerful form of leadership ability, skills, and decisions. Over the years, before my daddy passed away, he kept giving me instructions about many things concerning our first African American president BO. My daddy passed away when I was a junior at Florida Agricultural Mechanical University. My momma passed away ten years later.

The End

Index

A

Ansel Thompson, James, 6

B

Baldwin Junior and Senior High School, 7
BO, 4, 7
Bright, Fermon, 5

D

Daddy, 3–7
Daddy's prediction, 6–7
discrimination, 7
Duval Medical Center Hospital, 5

E

Edward Waters College, 7

F

Florida Agricultural Mechanical University, 6–7

G

Georg Ann, 5

H

HC, 4–5
HC's husband, 4, 7
Hester, Henry, 3–6
Hester, Peter. *See* Daddy
Hester, Ruby. *See* Momma
Hester, Sue Ann, 3–6
Hester Colleton-Akins, Jacquelyn, 3–4

J

Jacksonville, Florida, 3, 7
Jefferson Street, 5

M

Madison Street, 5
McCoy Boulevard, 3

Characters in the Story

1. Peter Hester (Daddy), deceased
2. Ruby Hester (Momma), deceased
3. Sue Ann Thompson (sister), consent
4. Henry Hester (uncle), deceased
5. Jacquelyn Hester Colleton-Akins
6. Lisa Thompson-Webb (niece), consent
7. Fermon Bright, deceased
8. James Ansel Thompson, deceased

Remarks

Stories are the universal method of teaching, having been used by humankind to communicate information and meaning since the beginning of time. This book will simultaneously involve the intellectual and emotional aspects of a person in learning in having a family time consisting of storytelling. My daddy opened this universe up to his children in stories.

Printed in the United States
By Bookmasters